$\mathcal{P}$ARLIN MEMORIAL LIBRARY

Everett, Massachusetts

In Memory of

Phineas & Mary Tobe

Hard and Soft

by Emily C. Dawson

amicus readers

Say hello to amicus readers.

You'll find our helpful dog, Amicus, chasing a ball—to let you know the reading level of a book.

A

Learn to Read

Frequent repetition of sentence structures, high frequency words, and familiar topics provide ample support for brand new readers. Approximately 100 words.

1

Read Independently

Repetition is mixed with varied sentence structures and 6 to 8 content words per book are introduced with photo label and picture glossary supports. Approximately 150 words.

2

Read to Know More

These books feature a higher text load with additional nonfiction features such as more photos, time lines, and text divided into sections. Approximately 250 words

Amicus Readers are published by Amicus
P.O. Box 1329, Mankato, Minnesota 56002
www.amicuspublishing.us

Printed in the United States of America at Corporate
Graphics, in North Mankato, Minnesota.

Series Editor   Rebecca Glaser
Series Designer   Christine Vanderbeek
Photo Researcher   Heather Dreisbach

Library of Congress Cataloging-in-Publication Data
Dawson, Emily C.
Hard and soft / by Emily C. Dawson.
p. cm. – (Amicus readers. Let's compare)
Includes bibliographical references and index.
Summary: "A level A Amicus Reader that compares
contrasts common hard and soft objects, both in nat
and man-made. Includes comprehension activity"–
Provided by publisher.
ISBN 978-1-60753-000-8 (library bound)
1. Matter–Properties–Juvenile literature.
2. Touch–Juvenile literature. 3. Polarity–Juvenile
literature. 4. Hardness–Juvenile literature. 5. English
language–Synonyms and antonyms. I. Title.
QC173.16.D385 2011
530.4'12–dc22
                                                           2011005.

Photo Credits
Ho Yeow Hui/iStockphoto, cover top; Anthony Rosenberg/iStockphoto, cover botom; Mallory Samson /GettyImages, 4; Peter38/Shutterst
6t; Lowe Llaguno/Shutterstock, 6b; Stephen Simpson/GettyImages, 8t; Sneekerp l Dreamstime.com, 8b; Tony Tremblay/iStockphoto, 10t;
arkanex/iStockphoto, 10b; greenland /Shutterstock, 12t; Fuse/GettyImages, 12b; Ty Allison/GettyImages, 14t; Cultura/GettyImages, 14
William Hart/GettyImages, 16; Marilyn Nieves/iStockphoto, 18; AHMAD FAIZAL YAHYA/iStockphoto, 20m; Hughstoneian l Dreamstime
20b; Elena Moiseeva l Dreamstime.com, 21t; Niels Quist Petersen/iStockphoto, 21b; VikaValter/iStockphoto, 22tl; Danny Smythe/iStockp
22ml; Fenykepez/iStockphoto, 22bl; Алексей Брагин/iStockphoto, 22tr; jaimie Duplass/Shutterstock, 22mr; David Morgan/iStockphoto,

1025   3-2011
10 9 8 7 6 5 4 3 2 1

Table of Contents

Black Rabbit 9-22-11 34, 25

**Let's compare
hard and soft.**
Hard things are strong
and firm. Soft things
move and squish.

hard

Let's Compare!

soft

6

Cars drive on the hard road. Mr. Ryan's car gets stuck in the soft mud.

hard

Let's Compare!

soft

8

Macy walks on the hard rocks. Jon lies in the soft grass.

hard

Let's Compare!

soft

10

Kids skate on the hard ice. Paul rests in the soft snow.

hard

Let's Compare!

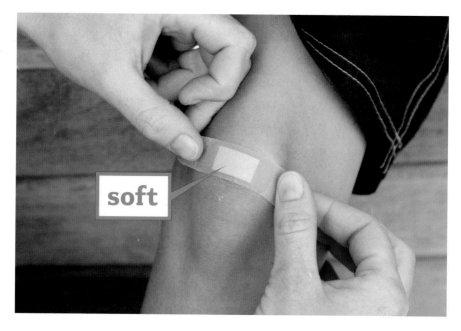

soft

12

Ethan fell on the hard sidewalk. A soft bandage helps his knee heal.

hard

Let's Compare!

soft

14

Alex runs on the hard track. Amy jumps on the soft mat.

Cole and Keisha's bunk beds are made of hard wood. Their blankets are made of soft cotton.

Hard things stay the same shape. Soft things bend. How do you use hard and soft things?

Picture Glossary

bandage →
a soft pad that covers
a scrape while it heals

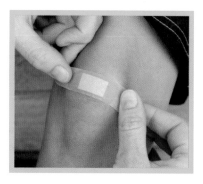

← **cotton**
soft cloth made from
the fluffy white fibers
of a plant

firm →
strong and not
able to bend

← squish
to change shape
when pressed

track →
a hard path for
running on

← wood
the hard material that
forms the trunk and
branches of a tree

Hard and Soft

Look at the photos.
 1. Which things are hard?
 2. Which things are soft?
 3. Which things do you use together?

Ideas for Parents and Teachers

Let's Compare, an Amicus Readers Level A series, gives children the opportunity to compare familiar concepts with lots of reading support. Repetitive sentence structures, familiar vocabulary, and photo labels reinforce concepts in the text. In each book, the picture glossary defines new vocabulary and the "Let's Compare" activity page reinforces compare and contrast techniques.

Before Reading
- Ask the child about the difference between hard and soft. Ask: What things are hard? What things are soft? How do you know?
- Discuss the cover photo. What do these photos tell them?
- Look at the picture glossary together. Read and discuss the words. Ask the child to sort the photos into a hard group and a soft group.

Read the Book
- "Walk" through the book and look at the photos. Ask questions or let the child ask questions about the photos.
- Read the book to the child or have him or her read independently.
- Show him or her how to read the photo labels and refer back to the picture glossary to understand the full meaning.

After Reading
- Have the child identify hard and soft things around the room.
- Prompt the child to think more, asking questions such as Why are some things hard and some things soft? Why is a library book hard? Why is a couch soft? Why are they made that way?

Let's Compare!

Index

Web Sites

Compare and Contrast Theme Page
http://www.enchantedlearning.com/themes/compare.shtml

Let's Make Sensory Books
http://content.scholastic.com/browse/article.jsp?id=3521